D0435992

WITHDRAWN

A Bird's-eye View of the Mansion, O

1. Mansion
2. Greenhouse and Quarters
3. Flower Garden
4. Icehouse
5. Museum
6. Botanical Garden
7. Spinning-House
8. Storehouse
9. Gardener's Ho
10. Office
11. Courtyard
12. Bowling Green

uildings and Gardens of Mount Vernon

The Children of
Mount Vernon

Nelly and George Washington Custis at Mt. Vernon

The Children of Mount Vernon

A GUIDE TO GEORGE WASHINGTON'S HOME

by Miriam Anne Bourne

Illustrated by Gloria Kamen

Doubleday & Company, Inc.
Garden City, New York
1981

Library of Congress Catalog Card Number 80–974
ISBN: 0-385-15534-4 Trade
ISBN: 0-385-15535-2 Prebound
Copyright © 1981 by the Mount Vernon Ladies' Association of the Union,
    Mount Vernon, Virginia
Printed in the United States of America
First edition

For FARN and IRENE

Contents

part **I**

"The Little Folks"

Introduction

George Washington was commander of the American army during the Revolutionary War. Later he became the first President of the United States.

Washington was also a farmer, even when he was busy being President and commander in chief. He farmed Mount Vernon plantation on the Potomac River in Virginia. Mount Vernon was divided into five farms.

Martha Washington lived at Mount Vernon with her husband. So did two of their grandchildren, Eleanor Parke Custis and George Washington Parke Custis. They were called Nelly and Wash.

The Custis children's father had died at the end of the Revolutionary War. That was when Wash and Nelly went to live with their Washington grandparents. The children loved being at Mount Vernon. Their older sisters Betsey and Patty came often to visit. So did their mother and numerous young cousins.

George Washington called Nelly and Wash the little folks. This story will help you discover where they played and what they did at Mount Vernon. It takes place in 1789, just before their grandfather became the first President.* Nelly was ten, and Wash was eight.

* Some of the furnishings in the story came to Mount Vernon after George Washington was President.

1 Chipmunk

The sound of carriage wheels in the courtyard woke Nelly up. Last night's guests must be leaving. Sunlight danced on the wallpaper. The smell of baking corn bread drifted through the windows. Nelly closed her eyes and tried to go back to sleep.

What if Wash remembered? Her brother had not wanted to give her the chipmunk he found yesterday. Nelly had begged and begged. At last Wash gave in.

"You'll have to find me a snake instead," he told his sister.

Make him forget that I promised, Nelly prayed silently.

She heard Wash run up the stairs.

"Careful, child!" called Dolly, one of the house servants. "You'll knock this laundry clean out of my arms."

There was a hammering on Nelly's door. She lay quietly in bed. As quiet as the chipmunk in the box hidden in her fireplace. Wash knocked again.

"You'll raise the dead," Dolly told him.

No use in trying to sleep. "Come in," Nelly called to her brother. Wash bounded into the room and up on the high bed.

"Get up, Nelly," he said. "Time to find me a snake." He jumped off the bed and ran into the hall.

His heavy boots pounded back down the stairs. Wash was "as full of spirits as an eggshell is of meat," Grandpapa always said.

Nelly put on her dress and kerchief and went down to the dining room. Grandpapa was having his corn bread and tea.

"Hurry, children," he said. "Mr. Lear is waiting in the schoolhouse. You must do your lessons before your sisters and cousins arrive for dinner." Mr. Lear was a tutor. Grandpapa had hired him to teach Nelly and Wash.

Nelly hurried past the gardener's house and through the gate to the flower garden. Tucked in a corner by itself was the little schoolhouse. Lessons might make Wash forget about the snake.

Wash walked slowly, scuffing his feet, making dust clouds in the air. He thought about the chipmunk. He had found it scratching for a nut between the roots of a big tree. It felt warm and soft when Wash held it in his hands. He could feel its tiny heartbeat. Wash wished it was still his.

But a snake would be fun. He could scare Dolly and his sisters with it. He could make Hercules the cook think he would drop it in the soup kettle. Wash stopped scuffing and ran to the schoolhouse.

As the spring day grew warm, Wash sat at the table figuring sums. While he worked, he watched two squirrels chase each other along the garden wall.

Nelly bent her head over her spelling book. But she peeked at the butterflies fluttering over a bed of tulips.

Wash practiced his penmanship. Would he ever be able to write his name grandly like Grandpapa? Wash stopped writing to watch a mockingbird hop down

from a bush. It tugged at a piece of string that tied a rose bush to a stake.

Outside the greenhouse, Judy and Lucy looked after the plantation children who were too young to work. They were all playing house.

Suddenly the gardener appeared and shooed them out of the garden.

"You'll break the shrubbery," he said crossly.

Mr. Lear read aloud from a book of fables in his flat New England speech. Nelly and Wash sighed. They were tired of sitting still. Their wooden chairs felt hard and uncomfortable.

Mr. Lear finished the fable and closed the book.

"Run along," he said cheerfully. "Did you know there are new puppies in the stable?"

Mr. Lear watched the children dash out of their chairs. He knew George Washington would approve.

"The little folks are too young to be long confined," he had told their tutor.

With one jump Wash cleared the schoolhouse steps. He ran through the garden and out the gate. Nelly skipped along behind him.

2 Thief

Dutchess watched uneasily as Wash cuddled her puppies. Big, shaggy Vulcan wagged his tail at Wash. He wanted to be patted too. Nelly reached in her pocket for the sugar from the sugar bowl in the parlor. She fed it to old Nelson. He was Grandpapa's horse during the war.

In the paddock the jackasses brayed and kicked up their heels. Vulcan went outside and barked at the jackasses.

Out on the river a barge horn blew. Dinner guests were arriving at the landing. It was almost three o'clock. A family carriage made its way from the west gate toward the mansion. Two strangers on horseback followed the carriage. Strangers often came to Mount Vernon to meet George Washington.

As the dinner bell clanged, Wash climbed onto Vulcan's broad back for a dash up the hill. "Giddyap!" he yelled.

Wash locked his arms around the big dog's neck. Past the coachhouse and the washhouse they ran. Past the smokehouse and the storehouse.

"He's forgotten about the snake," Nelly chuckled. She hurried up the hill to meet her mother and sisters and cousins.

Grandpapa stood tall by the west door greeting the visitors. To his relatives he gave a warm embrace. To the strangers he gave a reserved handshake. People came from all over to pay their respects to George Washington. He was a hero for winning America's independence from England. And soon Grandpapa would be President. He did not want to leave Mount Vernon. Grandpapa's boots were still muddy. Since breakfast he had ridden around his plantation.

When Grandmama heard the guests, she hurried over from the parlor to welcome them. Little cousin Maria came too, holding Grandmama's hand.

Vulcan saw his chance. Wash yelled as the dog ran into the kitchen and grabbed the dinner ham with his sharp teeth. Along the serpentine walks he raced, into the shrubberies, groves, and wildernesses.

"Oh no!" Grandmama cried. She stood on her tip-toes and clapped her hands in distress. Grandpapa threw back his head and roared with laughter.

Vulcan headed for the swamp. No one could catch him there. Fortunately, Grandmama had plenty of other food for dinner.

3 Hide and Seek

After dinner Wash and Nelly, their sisters Betsey and Patty, and their cousins played leap frog on the bowling green.

"Now we'll play hide-and-seek," Betsey announced. She pointed to a tree. "This is home base. I'm it." Betsey was thirteen. She was the oldest of the four Custis children.

"One a bin, two a bin,
three a bin, four,
Five a bin, six a bin,
seven give o'er.
A bunch of pins,
prick my shins.
A loaf of bread,
come knock me down.
I'm coming!"

Wash hid behind the ha-ha wall, which kept the cows off the lawn. He poked his head up over the edge to look for Betsey. Betsey saw him and raced back to home base.

Next time Wash hid in the low branches of an apple tree. Betsey caught him again.

The third time he ran into the kitchen garden. Without pausing, he tore past the vegetable beds and cisterns to the beehives. He crouched down behind them as the bees buzzed angrily. Wash peered around the hives toward the garden gate. No one in sight. Bent low, he scurried to the gardener's seed storehouse, up the steep steps and inside. He shut the door behind him.

Off in the distance he heard children's voices. "Keep in, keep in wherever you be!" Where was Betsey? Wash crouched down behind a barrel. If she opened the door, she would not be able to see him.

Wash listened intently. The gardener's hoe knocked against a rock. A crow cawed harshly. A breeze carried the smell of lye from the washhouse. There was no sound of his sisters and cousins.

"Maybe they've forgotten me," Wash thought unhappily. That was the trouble with being the youngest. Out in the fields the men and women called to each other. Wash wished someone would call to him. A seagull flew up from the river and mewed overhead. The seedhouse was warm. Wash's eyelids drooped. He rested his head on a seed bag and fell asleep.

Wash woke up with a start.

Someone was climbing the seedhouse steps!

It was Betsey. "There you are," she said when she saw Wash. She sank down onto the floor. She looked hot and tired. "I couldn't find anyone else."

Behind Betsey a small, green snake slid around a seed bag. Wash grinned. Betsey would jump if he showed her the snake. He reached out to grab it.

Suddenly the snake slithered across the floor.

"Oh!" Betsey cried. She jumped up. "What a cute little snake. Look at it, Wash. Isn't it a pretty one?"

Wash turned to his sister with surprise. Then he sprang to his feet to catch the snake.

"Don't, Wash," Betsey ordered. "It's mean to catch animals that want to be free." The snake squeezed through a hole and disappeared.

While Wash and Betsey were in the seedhouse, the other children stopped playing. The cousins saw Grandpapa riding home from his mill. They ran across the fields to meet him.

Nelly and her sister Patty had hidden by the old tomb. Then they ran the rest of the way down the hill to the boat landing.

"We don't care if Betsey can't find us," they said to each other. "She is too bossy." Patty was only one year younger than Betsey. But Patty was never bossy.

Out in the river a boat spread its sails to catch the light breeze. Jack and the other fishermen pulled at their nets. Along the shore long-legged birds waded. They were fishing too.

Nelly and Patty climbed back up the hill by the path through the woods. A blue jay scolded from a high branch. The roots of a huge tree sprawled over the ground. Was that where Wash had found the chipmunk? Nelly wondered. The roots would make a fine place for playing house.

"Let's show Betsey what we've found," Patty said. That was like Patty. She could never be cross with anyone for long.

4 Lost

At six o'clock the bell in the laundry yard rang for tea.
Wash and Betsey raced up the hill to the house. Grandmama and little Maria were in the hall.

"Maria says she saw a chipmunk in the house,"
Grandmama laughed.

"Nelly's chipmunk," Maria said.

"I told her animals live outside," Grandmama
said.

Maria stamped her little foot. "Chipmunk in
house!"

When Grandmama was gone, Wash went upstairs
to Nelly's room to check on the chipmunk.

"It's gone," he said when Nelly came in. "The
chipmunk isn't here."

"How do you know where I put the box?" Nelly
demanded.

Wash grinned. "I peeked through your keyhole
when you hid it." He stopped smiling. "The chipmunk
is gone," he said again.

"We will have to find it," Nelly said firmly. "After
tea you help me look."

When tea was over, the family gathered in the
parlor. Wash and Nelly whispered in the hall.

"Don't tell what we're looking for," Nelly warned
Wash, "or we'll be in trouble with Grandmama."

"I'll pretend I'm looking for my top," Wash told her.

There were few places on the first floor for a chipmunk to hide. In the banquet hall Wash and Nelly looked in the fireplace. No chipmunk.

It was not inside the closet under the stairs. It was nowhere in the dining room.

"There are too many people on this floor," Nelly whispered. "It would be afraid to hide here. Let's go upstairs."

On the second floor Nelly and Wash looked under beds and behind curtains. They looked inside Grandmama's trunk at the foot of the bed in Lafayette's room. Every winter during the war Grandmama had made the long trip to visit Grandpapa at army headquarters. In the spring she came home to Mount Vernon carrying presents in the trunk.

"I hope the chipmunk isn't hurt," Nelly said.

On the attic floor she and Wash checked the bedrooms. No chipmunk. They looked in the "lumber rooms" which were used for storage. No chipmunk.

"I hope it isn't dead," Nelly said.

Wash climbed the winding stairs to the cupola. There was no place to hide up there. But Wash liked to be in the cupola. Spread out below him was the Potomac River and all of Mount Vernon. Over the rippling fields swallows flitted. In the woods a woodpecker hammered on a dead tree. Wash wished he had left the chipmunk in the woods.

The children tiptoed down the stairs to the hall outside Grandmama's and Grandpapa's room. They looked in the door.

"It might be in the dressing room," Wash said.

His throat hurt. If the chipmunk were dead, it was his fault.

"It might be behind the doors of Grandmama's desk," Nelly said.

They dashed in for a quick look. No chipmunk.

"I should have told you to let it go," Nelly said.

They snuck downstairs to the library. There was no place there for a chipmunk to hide. Except the bookcase.

"Grandpapa will be angry if his books are nibbled," Wash said unhappily.

There were many places in the pantry for a chipmunk to hide. But there was no food or water for a hungry animal. Just dishes.

"There is nowhere else to look," Nelly said with a catch in her voice.

"Nelly," Wash said. "Never mind about finding me a snake."

Slowly the children walked back to their family.

5 Found!

Grandpapa stood outside on the piazza. Wash and Nelly went out to stand beside him. Grandpapa looked sad, as if he were thinking of leaving home. The children slipped a hand in his.

"No estate in United America is more pleasantly situated than Mount Vernon," Grandpapa said.

It was getting dark. Wherever you looked, fireflies blinked.

"Once I saw a toad," Grandpapa told Nelly and Wash. "It swallowed a firefly in one gulp. Would you believe it? That toad lit up like a lantern!"

Wash looked at Nelly. Did Nelly believe it? Grandpapa might be teasing.

Nelly was looking at Grandpapa. He was watching something. Down in the deer park stood a doe. Her two fawns grazed trustingly by her side. A buck joined the doe and fawns. The moon gleamed on his huge antlers.

Wash sensed a movement behind him. He looked around. In the open door was a chipmunk. Its nose twitched as it sniffed the big outside. Wash willed Nelly to look. As she did, the chipmunk stepped over the threshold and scurried off into the night.

Maria ran to the door.

"Nelly's chipmunk go bye-bye!" she said.

Grandpapa turned around.

"The chipmunks are asleep, Maria," he told her. "Come and see the deer."

Nelly and Wash smiled happily at each other. And another day ended at George Washington's Mount Vernon.

part II

The Plantation

Introduction

In George Washington's time Mount Vernon plantation was so big it took him all day to ride around its eight thousand acres. The Washington family lived at Mansion House Farm. The other four farms, which were nearby, were named Union, Dogue Run, River, and Muddy Hole.

They no longer exist. But Mansion House Farm looks very much as it did when Wash and Nelly lived there with their grandparents.

Nelly and Wash were not the only children at Mount Vernon with George and Martha Washington. It was home to Cousin Maria and her brothers and sisters too. Their mother and father helped run the plantation.

Mr. Lear lived in the mansion house. As well as being a tutor to the children, he was a secretary for Grandpapa.

There were also seventy-four slaves working for George and Martha Washington at Mansion House Farm. And there were 170 men, women, and children at the other four farms. By the time Washington died in 1799, there were even more. In his will, Washington set them all free.

Why did so many people work on the plantation? What did all of them do?

Spring

Fall

1
Farmers

Some people farmed. Every day George Washington rode around his plantation. In the spring he made sure workers plowed his fields and planted seeds. In the summer he made sure they hoed the weeds. In the fall he saw that they harvested crops. Who were all these field workers? Most of them were slaves. Each of the five plantation farms had an overseer who was in charge of the slaves.

Before Nelly and Wash were born, Grandpapa grew tobacco to sell. A cooper made barrels called hogsheads to hold the tobacco. The hogsheads were rolled down the hill to the boat landing. There they were loaded onto a schooner and sailed to market. The tobacco didn't make much money for Grandpapa.

His wheat growing was more successful. A miller ground the wheat into flour at George Washington's mill. Much of the flour was sold. Some of it was used by the plantation cooks to bake whole wheat bread and cakes and pastry.

Grandpapa also grew Indian corn. Some of the corn was ground into meal for hot corn bread. Grandpapa ate his with butter and honey. Much of the corn was fed to the farm animals.

Washington's Grist Mill

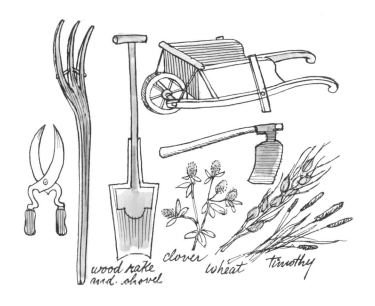

wood rake
and shovel

clover

wheat

timothy

Hay, oats, clover, and timothy were grown to feed Grandpapa's animals. Peas, potatoes, and turnips were grown to feed his workers.

Hemp and flax were planted too. Now who wants to eat those crops? Nobody. Hemp is twisted into rope. Flax and cotton are used for cloth. George Washington wanted cloth so clothes could be made on his plantation.

2
Spinners
and Weavers

Many of Grandpapa's and Wash's silver-sprigged waist-coats came from England. So did Grandmama's and Nelly's prettiest silk dresses. But their every day clothes and the workers' clothes were made on the plantation.

In the spinning and weaving house, girls spun thread from flax, cotton, and sheep fleece. It was not easy to learn to spin. The youngest girls felt as if their fingers were "all thumbs."

Weavers wove the spun thread into linen, cotton, wool, and linsey-woolsey cloth. Linsey-woolsey? That was linen and wool woven together. It made warm but scratchy coverlets for beds.

Betty, Lame Alice, and Charlotte were seamstresses. They snipped and sewed the woven cloth into men's clothes. Shirts and coats and breeches took shape under their nimble fingers. They made petticoats, skirts, and blouses for women. With tiny stitches they sewed ruffles for Wash's shirts. Some of the cloth they made into towels and napkins. And knitters knit yarn into mittens, sweaters, and stockings for the workers.

In the mansion house Grandmama spent cold winter evenings knitting for her family. She taught Nelly to do needlework. While they worked, fires burned in the fireplaces. Countless cords of wood had to be chopped to keep the house warm all winter.

weaving cloth

cutting the
finished cloth

sewing

mixing fats and potash

Soap-making

cutting soap into bars

dip candles

Candle-making

a candle-mold

hickory twigs and birch brooms

3
Housekeepers

"You must have the house well cleaned," George Washington once wrote his overseer. "You must get the chairs and tables well rubbed. The staircase ought also to be polished." Grandpapa and Grandmama always wanted Mount Vernon to sparkle.

But before a house servant could sweep a carpet, someone had to make a broom. Before a servant could scrub a floor, someone had to make a brush. Before a servant could polish the silver, someone had to make the polish. Living on a plantation was like being on an island. Almost everything you needed had to come from the plantation itself.

To wash Mount Vernon's lovely china and glassware, someone had to make soap. Soap was needed to scrub the family's clothes and bed linen. It was made with ashes and grease. What a tiresome, smelly job!

Candle dipping and molding was another job that seemed to take forever. Pieces of hemp were tied onto rods and dipped into hot fat. Or fat was poured into tin molds to make the candles.

There were no bathrooms in houses in George Washington's time. A servant filled a pitcher with hot water for shaving and bathing. A servant emptied chamber pots. There were always guests at Mount Ver-

Brickmaking

← *a brick mold*

squeezing excess clay from the mold

stacking wet bricks

non. House servants like Dolly had to change a lot of beds.

When Grandpapa wanted work done on his house, he had his own workmen. The painters had to make their own paint. The blacksmith had to make and repair iron tools. Workers had to dig clay for the brickmakers. The brickmakers had to shape and fire the clay into bricks.

The stones on the piazza came from England, but were laid by Mount Vernon workers. And one fall day Grandpapa stopped his work to watch a man fasten a new weather vane to the top of the cupola. A dove of peace swung over Mount Vernon.

The Blacksmith Shop

making nails
from square
rods

a hand-made nail

The Flower Garden

the schoolhouse in the garden

4
Gardeners

The trees and shrubs around the mansion house did not plant themselves. Workers dug holes in the ground and put them in. Walls and fences were built, and gravel and brick walks were laid. Someone planted the scarlet honeysuckle vine which climbs the colonnades.

George Washington's gardeners planted the box-wood and the rose bushes in the flower garden. They planted the flowers that Martha Washington picked for the house. There were snapdragon and foxglove and black-eyed susan. There were candytuft, forget-me-not, and sweet william catchfly.

When cold weather came, Nelly and Wash watched the gardeners carry into the greenhouse the potted plants and trees sent to Grandpapa from warm countries. Virginia winters were too chilly for such plants to live outside. They watched servants make sweet-smelling toilet water from the petals of roses.

The Kitchen

churning butter

5
Cooks

When her family wanted dinner, how did Grandmama get food? It was a full-time job. She needed a lot of people to help.

At "killing time" cattle and hogs had to be slaughtered. They were smoked in the smokehouse to keep from spoiling. Wild ducks and other game were smoked in the smokehouse too. Chickens and sheep were killed just before Hercules and Nathan cooked them.

Jack and the other fishermen cast nets into the river and caught fish. Much of the fish was sold or given to the workers. Some was salted to keep until Grandmama wanted fish for dinner.

Every day she visited the work places near the mansion house. At the hen house she had eggs collected for baking. (Grandmama's "Great Cake" used forty eggs!) At the barn the milkmaid milked cows. At the dairy a woman churned cream into butter.

Food was kept from spoiling with ice from the icehouse. On the coldest winter days workers cut blocks of ice from the river. Oxen dragged them across the snow to the icehouse. They were covered with sawdust and straw to make them last through warm weather.

In the kitchen garden the gardener and his helpers planted vegetables and herbs. They pruned and grafted

The Icehouse

(The present icehouse was built in the 1800's)

fruit trees to grow better fruit. Some trees were trained to climb over fences and walls. Grapevines and raspberry, gooseberry, and currant bushes were cared for. Beehives were tended, so the contented bees would make honey.

When the fruits and vegetables were ripe, servants preserved them. They made sweet, sticky jams from berries and fruit. They made relish and pickles from cucumbers, onions, and green tomatoes. They sliced and strung apples to dry for cooking later.

In the fall Wash and Nelly watched workers press apples into cider and grapes into wine. Nuts were gathered from walnut and chestnut trees. Honey was squeezed from the honeycombs which the bees had made.

What a lot of work for food! Then it had to be cooked and served. Someone had to get up early to tend

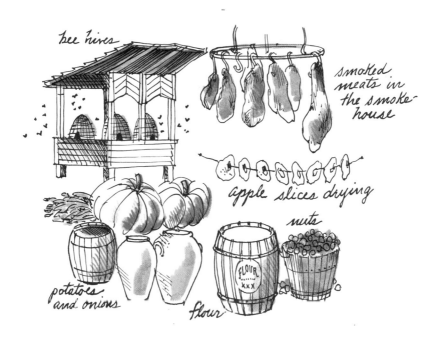

bee hives

smoked meats in the smoke-house

apple slices drying

nuts

potatoes and onions

flour

the fire that heated the oven. Someone had to chop the wood to feed the fire.

That wasn't all. If Wash was thirsty, he couldn't just turn a spigot for water. There was no plumbing to carry water into the house. Instead, he went to the well beside the kitchen. He lowered the bucket and drew it back up. The cold, spring water tasted good on hot, summer days.

6
Working Animals

If you like animals, you would have liked George Washington's plantation. There were horses, jackasses, mules and oxen, sheep, cattle, poultry, hogs, cats and dogs. The draft animals pulled the plows that turned over the fields. They hauled carts and wagons about the plantation. A horse carried Grandpapa when he visited his farms or went fox hunting. A special team of horses drew the Washington carriage when the family went to church. A blacksmith made iron shoes for the draft animals.

The sheep's fleece was shorn to make woolen clothes. Sheep and lambs were eaten. And sometimes sheep were Mount Vernon's lawn mowers They chomped on the grass that grew around the mansion house.

Poultry and hogs provided eggs, chicken, bacon, and ham. Cattle gave milk and beef. A shoemaker shaped leather from cattle hides into shoes and boots for people.

Cats lived in the barns and mill. They caught the mice that nibbled the grain.

And the plantation dogs? Did they have work to do? Dutchess and Vulcan were hound dogs. So were Ragman, Sweetlips, and Rover. They helped Grandpapa when he went hunting. Grandmama's coach dog ran alongside when she rode in the carriage. He kept wild animals out of the way.

The plantation puppies were the busiest dogs of all. They were busy playing with each other and with the children at Mount Vernon.

part *III*

Visiting Mount Vernon Today

Someday you may go to Mount Vernon. It is just a few miles from Washington, D.C. If you do, you can see where Wash and Nelly went to school and cuddled the puppies. You can see where they played hide-and-seek and looked for the lost chipmunk.

You can also play a game. As you walk around the plantation and mansion house, look for the objects on the next two pages. Can you find them? Where? The pictures on pages fifty-four and fifty-five will help.

Near Mount Vernon are George Washington's mill, his churches (Pohick Church and Christ Church), and the houses Nelly and Wash lived in when they grew up (Woodlawn and Arlington House, also known as the Custis-Lee Mansion).

George Washington loved his home. It is easy to understand why he told Nelly and Wash, "No estate in United America is more pleasantly situated than Mount Vernon."

 ○

1. weather
vane

 ○

2. mantel animals

 ○

3. shoe
lasts

 ○

4. fire buckets

 ○

5. hunting
horn

 ○

6. sun
spectacles

 ○

7. Toby
jug

 ○

8. iron

 ○

9. harpsichord

 ○

10. dogs on hearth

 ○

11. crib

 ○

12. plantation bell

○

13. rocking
horse

 ○

14. coach
jack

 ○

15. playing
cards

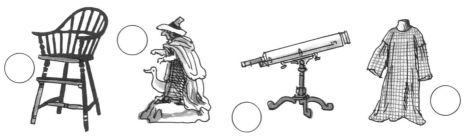

16. highchair   **17.** Mother Goose Figurine   **18.** telescope   **19.** bathing dress

20. knitting basket   **21.** fish hooks and toothbrush   **22.** globe   **23.** key to French prison

CAN YOU FIND THESE OBJECTS WHILE YOU ARE AT MOUNT VERNON?

Match the objects shown above with the rooms listed below. Write the correct letter in the circle next to each object.

A	shoemaker's room	**J**	banquet hall
B	servants' quarters (spinning house)	**K**	center hall
		L	west parlor
C	museum	**M**	little parlor
D	stable	**N**	dining room
E	washhouse	**O**	hall bedroom
F	laundry yard	**P**	Nelly's bedroom
G	kitchen	**Q**	Washingtons' bedroom
H	cupola	**R**	library
I	downstairs bedroom		

ANSWERS ON PAGE 56.

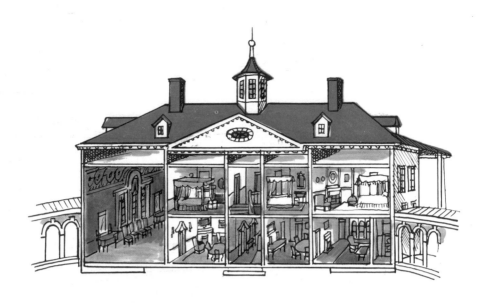

West Front View of the Mansion

Second-floor Rooms (left to right)

Banquet Hall
Blue Bedroom
Upper Hall
Nelly Custis's Bedroom
George and Martha Washingtons' Bedroom

First-floor Rooms (left to right)

Banquet Hall
West Parlor
Lower Hall
Dining Room
Library

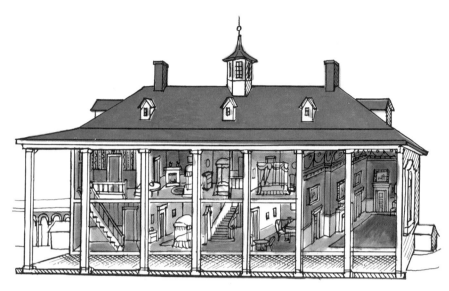

River Front View of the Interior of the Mansion

Second-floor Rooms (left to right)

Back Hall
Yellow Bedroom
Hall Bedroom
Stairs to Third Floor
Lafayettes' Bedroom

First-floor Rooms (left to right)

Back Stairs
Downstairs Bedroom
Central Hall
Little Parlor
Banquet Hall

A Washington, D.C., resident, Miriam Anne Bourne has long been intrigued with the children of the U.S. presidents and how their lives compared with those of most American children. *The Children of Mount Vernon* and four other books grew out of this interest. Aside from her writing career, Ms. Bourne is the founder and owner of a unique children's bookstore in the Washington, D.C., area which mails books to people all over the United States and abroad.

Gloria Kamen started her artistic career as a conceptual artist at the age of nine, making elaborate chalk drawings on the street in front of her apartment house in Brooklyn. She has been illustrating ever since, with twenty-five books and over one hundred children's stories to her credit. Ms. Kamen has also done a series of award-winning educational television programs for children in the Washington, D.C., area.

Answers to game on pages 52 and 53.

1 – H; 2 – J; 3 – A; 4 – Q; 5 – R; 6 – C; 7 – G; 8 – E; 9 – M; 10 – J; 11 – P;
12 – F; 13 – B; 14 – D; 15 – L; 16 – N; 17 – O; 18 – R; 19 – C; 20 – I;
21 – C; 22 – R; 23 – K

A Bird's-eye View of the Mansion, O

1. Mansion
2. Greenhouse and Quarters
3. Flower Garden
4. Icehouse
5. Museum
6. Botanical Garden
7. Spinning-House
8. Storehouse
9. Gardener's Ho
10. Office
11. Courtyard
12. Bowling Gree

uildings and Gardens of Mount Vernon

13. Kitchen
14. Butler's House
15. Smokehouse
16. Laundry Yard

17. Washhouse
18. Coachhouse
19. Kitchen Garden
20. Stable

21. Paddock
22. Park
23. Potomac River